To Clara

Happy Christmas

from the

Farnham Owens

Garry

We are all in the gutter, but some of us
are looking at the stars.
Oscar Wilde

First published in Great Britain in 2018 by

Quercus Editions Ltd
Carmelite House
50 Victoria Embankment
London EC4Y 0DZ

An Hachette UK company

A CIP catalogue record for this book is available
from the British Library

ISBN 978 1 78747 103 0

14

Typeset by Libanus Press, Marlborough
Printed and bound in Great Britain by Clays Ltd, Elcograf S.p.A.

POEMS

for a

WORLD

GONE

to

SH*T

Quercus

Okay, so giving you a book of poetry when the world feels like it's falling apart might seem a little bit 'answer blowing in the wind'.

But, as John Milton said:

'The mind is its own place,
and in itself can make a heaven of hell,
a hell of heaven.'

What he meant was:
sh*t happens.
It's how we react that makes the difference.

There are poets in this anthology who were writing centuries ago. And you know? They lived through some pretty serious sh*t. They felt f**ked off about the way the world was going, too. They just put it in prettier words.

So maybe reading what they had to say will help.

Here in this little book you will find inspiration to guide you through, from that first instinct to just get the f**k away from it all, via what the hell you can do about any of it, to realizing that the birds are still singing.

These poems are about remembering to keep looking up at the stars, whatever sh*t life is throwing at you.

I

what the f**k?

II

get me the f**k out of here . . .

III

keep your sh*t together

IV

let's do something about this sh*t

V

life is still f**king beautiful

I

what the f**k?

They fuck you up, your mum and dad.
    They may not mean to, but they do.
They fill you with the faults they had
    And add some extra, just for you.

But they were fucked up in their turn
    By fools in old-style hats and coats,
Who half the time were soppy-stern
    And half at one another's throats.

Man hands on misery to man.
    It deepens like a coastal shelf.
Get out as early as you can,
    And don't have any kids yourself.

from *macbeth*
william shakespeare

Tomorrow, and tomorrow, and tomorrow,
Creeps in this petty pace from day to day,
To the last syllable of recorded time;
And all our yesterdays have lighted fools
The way to dusty death. Out, out, brief candle!
Life's but a walking shadow, a poor player,
That struts and frets his hour upon the stage,
And then is heard no more. It is a tale
Told by an idiot, full of sound and fury,
Signifying nothing.

autumn love
li ch'ing-chao
translated by kenneth rexroth

Search. Search. Seek. Seek.
Cold. Cold. Clear. Clear.
Sorrow. Sorrow. Pain. Pain.
Hot flashes. Sudden chills.
Stabbing pains. Slow agonies.
I can find no peace
I drink two cups, then three bowls,
Of clear wine until I can't
Stand up against a gust of wind.
Wild geese fly over head.
They wrench my heart.
They were our friends in the old days.
Gold chrysanthemums litter
The ground, pile up, faded, dead.
This season I could not bear
To pick them up. All alone,
Motionless at my window,
I watch the gathering shadows.
Fine rain sifts through the wu-t'ung trees,
And drips, drop by drop, through the dusk.
What can I ever do now?
How can I drive off this word –
Hopelessness?

No sun – no moon!
    No morn – no noon –
No dawn –
    No sky – no earthly view –
    No distance looking blue –
No road – no street – no 't'other side the way' –
    No end to any Row –
    No indications where the Crescents go –
    No top to any steeple –
No recognitions of familiar people –
    No courtesies for showing 'em –
    No knowing 'em!
No travelling at all – no locomotion,
No inkling of the way – no notion –
    'No go' – by land or ocean –
    No mail – no post –
    No news from any foreign coast –
No park – no ring – no afternoon gentility –
    No company – no nobility –
No warmth, no cheerfulness, no healthful ease,
  No comfortable feel in any member –
No shade, no shine, no butterflies, no bees,
No fruits, no flowers, no leaves, no birds,
    November!

It was an evening in November.
As I very well remember,
I was strolling down the street in drunken pride,
But my knees were all a-flutter,
And I landed in the gutter
And a pig came up and lay down by my side.

Yes, I lay there in the gutter
Thinking thoughts I could not utter,
When a colleen passing by did softly say
'You can tell a man who boozes
By the company he chooses' –
And the pig got up and slowly walked away.

It's not that you're rich, it's that you're really fucking rich
like three holidays a year is not that dear, really rich
like you have that ruddy winter tan from sun-soaked
Bahamas trips in December just 'you know, to get a bit
of heat' really rich.
It's that your student loan was put into an isa really rich.
And uni fees were less than your school fees really rich.
And you've never waited tables or been a till assistant rich
because at weekends you drove to see the Hiltons really rich

So when you say that the change of soup kitchen laws is
necessary, that giving a free bowl of soup should be banned
because it encourages people to choose a homeless life of
freezing cold streets, the humiliation of begging for food,
money or help and the constant danger of sleeping rough I
just can't help thinking I've had enough. I can't even be arsed
to rhyme if these are the people leading the country.

Fuck.

We wear the mask that grins and lies,
It hides our cheeks and shades our eyes, –
This debt we pay to human guile;
With torn and bleeding hearts we smile,
And mouth with myriad subtleties.

Why should the world be over-wise,
In counting all our tears and sighs?
Nay, let them only see us, while
    We wear the mask.

We smile, but, O great Christ, our cries
To thee from tortured souls arise.
We sing, but oh the clay is vile
Beneath our feet, and long the mile;
But let the world dream otherwise,
    We wear the mask!

from *differences of opinion*
wendy cope

He tells her that the earth is flat –
He knows the facts, and that is that.
In altercations fierce and long
She tries her best to prove him wrong.
But he has learned to argue well.
He calls her arguments unsound
And often asks her not to yell.
She cannot win. He stands his ground.

The planet goes on being round.

Water, water, every where,
And all the boards did shrink;
Water, water, every where,
Nor any drop to drink.

The very deep did rot: O Christ!
That ever this should be!
Yea, slimy things did crawl with legs
Upon the slimy sea.

Why
Can't
Heads
Have
Overflow pipes
     Like toilets?
     If
     They
     Did
     I
     Could
     Pull
     My
     Ear
     And
     Flush
     It
     All
     Out.

What trifling coil do we poor mortals keep;
Wake, eat, and drink, evacuate, and sleep.

from *the hollow men*
t. s. eliot

This is the way the world ends
This is the way the world ends
This is the way the world ends
Not with a bang but a whimper.

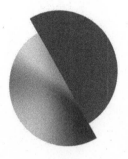

II

get me the f**k out of here . . .

Away, away, from men and towns,
To the wild wood and the downs –
To the silent wilderness
Where the soul need not repress
Its music lest it should not find
An echo in another's mind,
While the touch of Nature's art
Harmonizes heart to heart.

from *the ship of death*
d. h. lawrence

O let us talk of quiet that we know,
that we can know, the deep and lovely quiet
of a strong heart at peace!

How can we this, our own quietus, make?

I will arise and go now, and go to Innisfree,
And a small cabin build there, of clay and wattles made:
Nine bean-rows will I have there, a hive for the honey-bee,
And live alone in the bee-loud glade.

And I shall have some peace there, for peace comes dropping
    slow,
Dropping from the veils of the morning to where the cricket
    sings;
There midnight's all a glimmer, and noon a purple glow,
And evening full of the linnet's wings.

I will arise and go now, for always night and day
I hear lake water lapping with low sounds by the shore;
While I stand on the roadway, or on the pavements grey,
I hear it in the deep heart's core.

the way through the woods
rudyard kipling

They shut the road through the woods
      Seventy years ago.
Weather and rain have undone it again,
      And now you would never know
There was once a road through the woods
      Before they planted the trees.
It is underneath the coppice and heath
      And the thin anemones.
Only the keeper sees
      That, where the ring-dove broods,
And the badgers roll at ease,
      There was once a road through the woods.

Yet, if you enter the woods
  Of a summer evening late,
When the night-air cools on the trout-ringed pools
  Where the otter whistles his mate,
(They fear not men in the woods,
  Because they see so few.)
You will hear the beat of a horse's feet,
  And the swish of a skirt in the dew,
Steadily cantering through
  The misty solitudes,
As though they perfectly knew
  The old lost road through the woods . . .
But there is no road through the woods.

My soul is awakened, my spirit is soaring
    And carried aloft on the wings of the breeze;
For above and around me the wild wind is roaring,
    Arousing to rapture the earth and the seas.

The long withered grass in the sunshine is glancing,
    The bare trees are tossing their branches on high;
The dead leaves beneath them are merrily dancing,
    The white clouds are scudding across the blue sky.

I wish I could see how the ocean is lashing
    The foam of its billows to whirlwinds of spray;
I wish I could see how its proud waves are dashing,
    And hear the wild roar of their thunder to-day!

the oldest reason in the world
gil scott-heron

. . . because i always feel like running.
not away,
. . . because there's no such place.
. . . because if there was
i would have found it by now
. . . because it's easier to run; easier than staying
and finding out you're the only one who didn't run
. . . because running will be the way your life and mine
will be described:
as in the long run or
as in having given someone a run for his money or
as in running out of time
. . . because running makes me look like everyone else
though i hope there will never
be cause for that
. . . because i will be running in the other direction:
not running for cover;
. . . because if i knew where cover was
i would stay there and never have to run for it.
not running for my life
. . . because i have to be running
for something of more value to be running

and not in fear;
. . . because the thing i fear cannot be
escaped, eluded, avoided,
   hidden from, protected from, gotten away from,
   not without showing the fear
   as i see it now
      . . . because closer, clearer/no sir nearer
      . . . because of you, and
      . . . because of the nice that you
   quietly, quickly be causing and
      . . . because you're going to see me run soon, and
      . . . because you're going to know why i'm running.
   then.
   you'll know then
      . . . because i'm not going to tell you now.

I plan to construct a secret glass dome,
beautiful to the human, lizard or giant isopod eye.

Think of it as a kind of survival curation,
a large hot house built for the future.

Some walls will house aquariums of angel fish.
Other walls will play videos of teen

movies from 1990s, e.g. *Pump Up the Volume*
through a fronded canopy of tropical trees,

home to toucans, soda streams and religious
iconography. The things I want to preserve

forever in a controlled climate, after the Arctic,
like a poem the size of a basketball court.

Here,
　　With my beer
I sit,
While golden moments flit:
　　Alas!
　　They pass
Unheeded by:
And, as they fly,
I,
Being dry,
　　Sit, idly sipping here
　　My beer.

He pored upon the leaves, and on the flowers,
   And heard a voice in all the winds; and then
He thought of wood-nymphs and immortal bowers,
   And how the goddesses came down to men:
He miss'd the pathway, he forgot the hours,
   And when he look'd upon his watch again,
He found how much old Time had been a winner –
He also found that he had lost his dinner.

Here lies a poor woman who was always tired,
She lived in a house where help wasn't hired:
Her last words on earth were: 'Dear friends, I am going
To where there's no cooking, or washing, or sewing,
For everything there is exact to my wishes,
For where they don't eat there's no washing of dishes.
I'll be where loud anthems will always be ringing,
But having no voice I'll be quit of the singing.
Don't mourn for me now, don't mourn for me never,
I am going to do nothing for ever and ever.'

Does the road wind up-hill all the way?
    Yes, to the very end.
Will the day's journey take the whole long day?
    From morn to night, my friend.

But is there for the night a resting-place?
    A roof for when the slow dark hours begin.
May not the darkness hide it from my face?
    You cannot miss that inn.

Shall I meet other wayfarers at night?
    Those who have gone before.
Then must I knock, or call when just in sight?
    They will not keep you standing at that door.

Shall I find comfort, travel-sore and weak?
    Of labour you shall find the sum.
Will there be beds for me and all who seek?
    Yea, beds for all who come.

A long – long Sleep – A famous – Sleep –
That makes no show for Morn –
By Stretch of Limb – or stir of Lid –
An independent One –

Was ever idleness like This?
Upon a Bank of Stone
To bask the Centuries away –
Nor once look up – for Noon?

III

keep your sh*t together

Sigh no more, ladies, sigh no more,
    Men were deceivers ever,
One foot in sea, and one on shore,
    To one thing constant never.
Then sigh not so, but let them go,
    And be you blithe and bonny,
Converting all your sounds of woe
    Into hey nonny nonny.

Sing no more ditties, sing no more
    Of dumps so dull and heavy,
The fraud of men was ever so
    Since summer first was leafy.
Then sigh not so, but let them go,
    And be you blithe and bonny,
Converting all your sounds of woe
    Into hey nonny nonny.

In the very early morning
Long before Dawn time
I lay down in the paddock
And listened to the cold song of the grass.
Between my fingers the green blades,
And the green blades pressed against my body.
'Who is she leaning so heavily upon me?'
Sang the grass.
'Why does she weep on my bosom,
Mingling her tears with the tears of my mystic lover?
Foolish little earth child!
It is not yet time.
One day I shall open my bosom
And you shall slip in – but not weeping.
Then in the early morning
Long before Dawn time
Your lover will lie in the paddock.
Between his fingers the green blades
And the green blades pressed against his body . . .
My song shall not sound cold to him
In my deep wave he will find the wave of your hair
In my strong sweet perfume, the perfume of your kisses.
Long and long he will lie there . . .
Laughing – not weeping.'

The days, the days they break to fade.
What fills them I'll forget.
Every touch and smell and taste.
This sun, about to set

can never last. It breaks my heart.
Each joy feels like a threat:
Although there's beauty everywhere,
its shadow is regret.

Still, something in the coming dusk
whispers not to fret.
Don't matter that we'll lose today.
It's not tomorrow yet.

the edge
lola ridge

I

I thought to die that night in the solitude
      where they would never find me . . .
But there was time . . .
And I lay quietly on the drawn knees of the mountain,
      staring into the abyss.

I do not know how long . . .
I could not count the hours, they ran so fast –
Like little bare-foot urchins – shaking my hands away.
But I remember
Somewhere water trickled like a thin severed vein . . .
And a wind came out of the grass,
Touching me gently, tentatively, like a paw.

As the night grew
The gray cloud that had covered the sky like sackcloth
Fell in ashen folds about the hills,
Like hooded virgins pulling their cloaks about them . . .
There must have been a spent moon,
For the tall one's veil held a shimmer of silver . . .

This too I remember,
And the tenderly rocking mountain,

Silence,
And beating stars . . .

II

Dawn
Lay like a waxen hand upon the world,
And folded hills
Broke into a solemn wonder of peaks stemming clear and cold,
Till the Tall One bloomed like a lily,
Flecked with sun
Fine as a golden pollen –
It seemed a wind might blow it from the snow.

I smelled the raw sweet essence of things,
And heard spiders in the leaves,
And ticking of little feet
As tiny creatures came out of their doors
To see God pouring light into his star . . .

. . . It seemed life held
No future and no past for me but this . . .

And I too got up stiffly from the earth,
And held my heart up like a cup . . .

The moment when, after many years
of hard work and a long voyage
you stand in the centre of your room,
house, half-acre, square mile, island, country,
knowing at last how you got there,
and say, I own this,

is the same moment when the trees unloose
their soft arms from around you,
the birds take back their language,
the cliffs fissure and collapse,
the air moves back from you like a wave
and you can't breathe.

No, they whisper. You own nothing.
You were a visitor, time after time
climbing the hill, planting the flag, proclaiming.
We never belonged to you.
You never found us.
It was always the other way round.

Your children are not your children.
They are the sons and daughters of Life's longing for itself.
They come through you but not from you,
And though they are with you, yet they belong not to you.

You may give them your love but not your thoughts,
For they have their own thoughts.
You may house their bodies but not their souls,
For their souls dwell in the house of tomorrow,
Which you cannot visit, not even in your dreams.
You may strive to be like them,
But seek not to make them like you.
For life goes not backward nor tarries with yesterday.

You are the bows from which your children
As living arrows are sent forth.
The archer sees the mark upon the path of the infinite,
And He bends you with His might
That His arrows may go swift and far.
Let your bending in the archer's hand be for gladness;
For even as He loves the arrow that flies,
So He loves also the bow that is stable.

chaplinesque
hart crane

We make our meek adjustments,
Contented with such random consolations
As the wind deposits
In slithered and too ample pockets.

For we can still love the world, who find
A famished kitten on the step, and know
Recesses for it from the fury of the street,
Or warm torn elbow coverts.

We will sidestep, and to the final smirk
Dally the doom of that inevitable thumb
That slowly chafes its puckered index toward us,
Facing the dull squint with what innocence
And what surprise!

And yet these fine collapses are not lies
More than the pirouettes of any pliant cane;
Our obsequies are, in a way, no enterprise.
We can evade you, and all else but the heart:
What blame to us if the heart live on.

The game enforces smirks; but we have seen
The moon in lonely alleys make
A grail of laughter of an empty ash can,
And through all sound of gaiety and quest
Have heard a kitten in the wilderness.

Men say they know many things;
But lo! they have taken wings, –
The arts and sciences,
And a thousand appliances;
The wind that blows
Is all that any body knows.

I'm Nobody! Who are you?
Are you – Nobody – Too?
Then there's a pair of us?
Don't tell! they'd advertise – you know!

How dreary – to be – Somebody!
How public – like a Frog –
To tell one's name – the livelong June –
To an admiring Bog!

the consolation
anne brontë

Though bleak these woods, and damp the ground
With fallen leaves so thickly strown,
And cold the wind that wanders round
With wild and melancholy moan;

There *is* a friendly roof, I know,
Might shield me from the wintry blast;
There is a fire, whose ruddy glow
Will cheer me for my wanderings past.

And so, though still, where'er I go,
Cold stranger-glances meet my eye;
Though, when my spirit sinks in woe,
Unheeded swells the unbidden sigh;

Though solitude, endured too long,
Bids youthful joys too soon decay,
Makes mirth a stranger to my tongue,
And overclouds my noon of day;

When kindly thoughts, that would have way,
Flow back discouraged to my breast; –
I know there *is*, though far away,
A home where heart and soul may rest.

Warm hands are there, that, clasped in mine,
The warmer heart will not belie;
While mirth, and truth, and friendship shine
In smiling lip and earnest eye.

The ice that gathers round my heart
May there be thawed; and sweetly, then,
The joys of youth, that now depart,
Will come to cheer my soul again.

Though far I roam, that thought shall be
My hope, my comfort, everywhere;
While such a home remains to me,
My heart shall never know despair!

> *La noche buena se viene,*
> *La noche buena se va,*
> *Y nosotros nos iremos*
> *Y no volveremos mas.*
>   – Old Villancico

Sweet evenings come and go, love,
    They came and went of yore:
This evening of our life, love,
    Shall go and come no more.

When we have passed away, love,
    All things will keep their name;
But yet no life on earth, love,
    With ours will be the same.

The daisies will be there, love,
    The stars in heaven will shine:
I shall not feel thy wish, love,
    Nor thou my hand in thine.

A better time will come, love,
    And better souls be born:
I would not be the best, love,
    To leave thee now forlorn.

The songs I had are withered
Or vanished clean,
Yet there are bright tracks
Where I have been,

And there grow flowers
For others' delight.
Think well, O singer,
Soon comes night.

IV

let's do something about this sh*t

Your ancestors did not survive
everything that nearly ended them
for you to shrink yourself
to make someone else
comfortable.

This sacrifice is your warcry, be loud,
be everything and make them proud.

If you can keep your head when all about you
      Are losing theirs and blaming it on you;
If you can trust yourself when all men doubt you,
      But make allowance for their doubting too;
If you can wait and not be tired of waiting,
      Or being lied about, don't deal in lies,
Or being hated, don't give way to hating,
      And yet don't look too good, nor talk too wise:

If you can dream – and not make dreams your master;
      If you can think – and not make thought your aim;
If you can meet with Triumph and Disaster
      And treat those two impostors just the same;
If you can bear to hear the truth you've spoken
      Twisted by knaves to make a trap for fools,
Or watch the things you gave your life to, broken,
      And stoop and build 'em up with worn-out tools . . .

If you can talk with crowds and keep your virtue,
      Or walk with Kings – nor lose the common touch,
If neither foes nor loving friends can hurt you,
      If all men count with you, but none too much;
If you can fill the unforgiving minute
      With sixty seconds' worth of distance run,
Yours is the Earth and everything that's in it,
      And – which is more – you'll be a Man, my son!

Rise like Lions after slumber
In unvanquishable number,
Shake your chains to earth like dew
Which in sleep had fallen on you –
Ye are many – they are few.

I was angry with my friend:
I told my wrath, my wrath did end.
I was angry with my foe:
I told it not, my wrath did grow.

And I water'd it in fears,
Night & morning with my tears;
And I sunned it with smiles,
And with soft deceitful wiles.

And it grew both day and night,
Till it bore an apple bright;
And my foe beheld it shine,
And he knew that it was mine,

And into my garden stole
When the night had veil'd the pole:
In the morning glad I see
My foe outstretch'd beneath the tree.

To sin by silence, when we should protest,
Makes cowards out of men. The human race
Has climbed on protest. Had no voice been raised
Against injustice, ignorance, and lust,
The inquisition yet would serve the law,
And guillotines decide our least disputes.
The few who dare, must speak and speak again
To right the wrongs of many. Speech, thank God,
No vested power in this great day and land
Can gag or throttle. Press and voice may cry
Loud disapproval of existing ills;
May criticize oppression and condemn
The lawlessness of wealth-protecting laws
That let the children and childbearers toil
To purchase ease for idle millionaires.

Therefore I do protest against the boast
Of independence in this mighty land.
Call no chain strong, which holds one rusted link.
Call no land free, that holds one fettered slave.
Until the manacled slim wrists of babes
Are loosed to toss in childish sport and glee,
Until the mother bears no burden, save
The precious one beneath her heart, until
God's soil is rescued from the clutch of greed
And given back to labor, let no man
Call this the land of freedom.

still.i rise
maya angelou

You may write me down in history
With your bitter, twisted lies,
You may tread me in the very dirt
But still, like dust, I'll rise.

Does my sassiness upset you?
Why are you beset with gloom?
'Cause I walk like I've got oil wells
Pumping in my living room.

Just like moons and like suns,
With the certainty of tides,
Just like hopes springing high,
Still I'll rise.

Did you want to see me broken?
Bowed head and lowered eyes?
Shoulders falling down like teardrops.
Weakened by my soulful cries.

Does my haughtiness offend you?
Don't you take it awful hard
'Cause I laugh like I've got gold mines
Diggin' in my own backyard.

You may shoot me with your words,
You may cut me with your eyes,
You may kill me with your hatefulness,
But still, like air, I'll rise.

Does my sexiness upset you?
Does it come as a surprise
That I dance like I've got diamonds
At the meeting of my thighs?

Out of the huts of history's shame
I rise
Up from a past that's rooted in pain
I rise
I'm a black ocean, leaping and wide,
Welling and swelling I bear in the tide.

Leaving behind nights of terror and fear
I rise
Into a daybreak that's wondrously clear
I rise
Bringing the gifts that my ancestors gave,
I am the dream and the hope of the slave.
I rise
I rise
I rise.

If I can stop one Heart from breaking,
I shall not live in vain
If I can ease one Life the Aching
Or cool one Pain

Or help one fainting Robin
Unto his Nest again,
I shall not live in Vain.

In the coming year enfolded
    Bright and sad hours lie,
Waiting till you reach and live them
    As the year rolls by.

In the happy hours and radiant
    I would like to be
Somewhere out of sight, forgotten,
    Your delight to see.

But when you are tired and saddened,
    Vexed with life, dismayed,
I would steal your grief, and lay it
    Where my own is laid –

Bleed my heart out in your service
    If, set free from pain,
You, through me, found life worth living,
    Glad and fair again.

Out of your whole life give but a moment!
All of your life that has gone before,
All to come after it, – so you ignore,
So you make perfect the present, – condense,
In a rapture of rage, for perfection's endowment,
Thought and feeling and soul and sense –
Merged in a moment which gives me at last
You around me for once, you beneath me, above me –
Me – sure that despite of time future, time past, –
This tick of our life-time's one moment you love me!
How long such suspension may linger? Ah, Sweet –
The moment eternal – just that and no more –
When ecstasy's utmost we clutch at the core
While cheeks burn, arms open, eyes shut and lips meet!

Not to say what everyone else was saying
not to believe what everyone else believed
not to do what everybody did,
then to refute what everyone else was saying
then to disprove what everyone else believed
then to deprecate what everybody did,

was his way to come by understanding

how everyone else was saying the same as he was saying
believing what he believed
and did what doing.

autobiography in five chapters
portia nelson

I

I walk down the street.
There is a deep hole in the sidewalk
I fall in.
I am lost . . .
I am hopeless.
It isn't my fault.
It takes forever to find a way out.

II

I walk down the same street.
There is a deep hole in the sidewalk.
I pretend I don't see it.
I fall in again.
I can't believe I'm in the same place.
But it isn't my fault.
It still takes a long time to get out.

III

I walk down the same street.
There is a deep hole in the sidewalk.
I see it is there.
I still fall in . . . it's a habit
My eyes are open; I know where I am;
It is my fault.
I get out immediately.

IV

I walk down the same street.
There is a deep hole in the sidewalk.
I walk around it.

V

I walk down another street.

from *little things*
julia carney

Little deeds of kindness,
Little words of love,
Help to make earth happy
Like the Heaven above.

V

life is still f**king beautiful

Every day is a fresh beginning,
Listen my soul to the glad refrain.
And, spite of old sorrows
And older sinning,
Troubles forecasted
And possible pain,
Take heart with the day and begin again.

Tall nettles cover up, as they have done
These many springs, the rusty harrow, the plough
Long worn out, and the roller made of stone:
Only the elm butt tops the nettles now.

This corner of the farmyard I like most:
As well as any bloom upon a flower
I like the dust on the nettles, never lost
Except to prove the sweetness of a shower.

At the break of day
I wanted to be a heart.
A heart.

And at the twilight hour
I wanted to be a nightingale.
A nightingale.

Soul,
turn the colour of flames.
Soul,
turn the colour of love.

In the bright morning
I wanted to be myself.
A heart.

And in the late night
I wanted to be my voice.
A nightingale.

Soul,
turn the colour of flames.
Soul,
turn the colour of love.

a fine day
katherine mansfield

After all the rain, the sun
Shines on hill and grassy mead;
Fly into the garden, child,
You are very glad indeed.

For the days have been so dull,
Oh, so special dark and drear,
That you told me, 'Mr Sun
Has forgotten we live here.'

Dew upon the lily lawn,
Dew upon the garden beds;
Daintily from all the leaves
Pop the little primrose heads.

And the violets in the copse
With their parasols of green
Take a little peek at you;
They're the bluest you have seen.

On the lilac tree a bird
Singing first a little note,
Then a burst of happy song
Bubbles in his lifted throat.

O the sun, the comfy sun!
This the song that you must sing,
'Thank you for the birds, the flowers,
Thank you, sun, for everything.'

from *song of myself*
walt whitman

I exist as I am, that is enough,
If no other in the world be aware I sit content,
And if each and all be aware I sit content.

The smoke of my own breath,

Echoes, ripples, buzz'd whispers, love-root, silk-thread,
crotch and vine,

My respiration and inspiration, the beating of my heart,
the passing of blood and air through my lungs,

The sniff of green leaves and dry leaves, and of the shore,
and dark-color'd sea-rocks, and of hay in the barn,

The sound of the belch'd words of my voice loos'd to the
eddies of the wind,

A few light kisses, a few embraces, a reaching around
of arms,

The play of shine and shade on the trees as the supple
boughs wag,

The delight alone, or in the rush of the streets, or along the
fields and hill-sides,

The feeling of health, the full-noon trill, the song of me
rising from bed and meeting the sun.

Is it so small a thing
To have enjoy'd the sun,
To have lived light in the spring,
To have loved, to have thought, to have done;
To have advanced true friends, and beat down baffling foes?

I am myself at last; now I achieve
My very self, I, with the wonder mellow,
Full of fine warmth, I issue forth in clear
And single me, perfected from my fellow.

Here I am all myself. No rose-bush heaving
Its limpid sap to culmination has brought
Itself more sheer and naked out of the green
In stark-clear roses, than I to myself am brought.

for desire
kim addonizio

Give me the strongest cheese, the one that stinks best;
and I want the good wine, the swirl in crystal
surrendering the bruised scent of blackberries,
or cherries, the rich spurt in the back
of the throat, the holding it there before swallowing.
Give me the lover who yanks open the door
of his house and presses me to the wall
in the dim hallway, and keeps me there until I'm drenched
and shaking, whose kisses arrive by the boatload
and begin their delicious diaspora
through the cities and small towns of my body.
To hell with the saints, with martyrs
of my childhood meant to instruct me
in the power of endurance and faith,
to hell with the next world and its pallid angels
swooning and sighing like Victorian girls.
I want this world. I want to walk into
the ocean and feel it trying to drag me along
like I'm nothing but a broken bit of scratched glass,
and I want to resist it. I want to go
staggering and flailing my way
through the bars and back rooms,
through the gleaming hotels and weedy
lots of abandoned sunflowers and the parks
where dogs are let off their leashes

in spite of the signs, where they sniff each
other and roll together in the grass, I want to
lie down somewhere and suffer for love until
it nearly kills me, and then I want to get up again
and put on that little black dress and wait
for you, yes you, to come over here
and get down on your knees and tell me
just how fucking good I look.

The lights from the parlour and kitchen shone out
Through the blinds and the windows and bars;
And high overhead and moving about,
There were thousands of millions of stars.
There ne'er were such thousands of leaves on a tree,
Nor of people in church or the park,
As the crowds of the stars that looked down upon me,
And that glittered and winked in the dark.

The Dog, and the Plough, and the Hunter, and all,
And the star of the sailor, and Mars,
These shone in the sky, and the pail by the wall
Would be half full of water and stars.
They saw me at last, and they chased me with cries,
And they soon had me packed into bed;
But the glory kept shining and bright in my eyes,
And the stars going round in my head.

I

The Owl and the Pussy-cat went to sea
    In a beautiful pea-green boat,
They took some honey, and plenty of money,
    Wrapped up in a five-pound note.
The Owl looked up to the stars above,
    And sang to a small guitar,
'O lovely Pussy! O Pussy, my love,
    What a beautiful Pussy you are,
        You are,
        You are!
    What a beautiful Pussy you are!'

II

Pussy said to the Owl, 'You elegant fowl!
    How charmingly sweet you sing!
O let us be married! too long we have tarried:
    But what shall we do for a ring?'
They sailed away, for a year and a day,
    To the land where the Bong-tree grows
And there in a wood a Piggy-wig stood
    With a ring at the end of his nose,
        His nose,
        His nose,
    With a ring at the end of his nose.

III

'Dear Pig, are you willing to sell for one shilling
    Your ring?' Said the Piggy, 'I will.'
So they took it away, and were married next day
    By the Turkey who lives on the hill.
They dined on mince, and slices of quince,
    Which they ate with a runcible spoon;
And hand in hand, on the edge of the sand,
    They danced by the light of the moon,
      The moon,
      The moon,
    They danced by the light of the moon.

sci-fi
tracy k. smith

There will be no edges, but curves.
Clean lines pointing only forward.

History, with its hard spine & dog-eared
Corners, will be replaced with nuance,

Just like the dinosaurs gave way
To mounds and mounds of ice.

Women will still be women, but
The distinction will be empty. Sex,

Having outlived every threat, will gratify
Only the mind, which is where it will exist.

For kicks, we'll dance for ourselves
Before mirrors studded with golden bulbs.

The oldest among us will recognize that glow –
But the word *sun* will have been re-assigned

To the Standard Uranium-Neutralizing device
Found in households and nursing homes.

And yes, we'll live to be much older, thanks
To popular consensus. Weightless, unhinged,

Eons from even our own moon, we'll drift
In the haze of space, which will be, once

And for all, scrutable and safe.

Happy the man, and happy he alone,
He who can call today his own:
He who, secure within, can say,
Tomorrow do thy worst, for I have lived today.

Index of Poems, **Poets** and *First Lines*

Acknowledgements

Quercus Poetry gratefully acknowledges the following for their permission to reproduce copyright material:

Kim Addonizio, 'For Desire', from *Tell Me.* Copyright © 2000 by Kim Addonizio. Reprinted with the permission of The Permissions Company, Inc., on behalf of BOA Editions, Ltd., www.boaeditions.org

Maya Angelou, 'Still I Rise', copyright © Maya Angelou 1978. Reprinted by permission of Virago, an imprint of Little, Brown Book Group.

Margaret Atwood, 'The Moment', from *Morning in the Burned House*, reproduced with permission of Curtis Brown Group Ltd, London, on behalf of Margaret Atwood. Copyright © Margaret Atwood 1995.

Wendy Cope, 'Differences of Opinion', from *Family Values* (2011). Reprinted with permission of Faber and Faber Ltd.

Francine Elena, 'In Preparation for the End Times', originally published by Test Centre Seven magazine. Copyright © 2016 by Francine Elena. Reprinted with permission of Francine Elena.

T. S. Eliot, from *The Hollow Men*, from *The Complete Poems and Plays of T. S. Eliot.* Reprinted with permission of Faber and Faber Ltd.

Nikita Gill, 'Ancestors', copyright © Nikita Gill. Reproduced with kind permission of Nikita Gill.

Philip Larkin, 'This Be The Verse', from *High Windows*. Reprinted with permission of Faber and Faber Ltd.

Li Ch'ing-Chao, 'A Weary Song to a Slow Sad Tune', translated by Kenneth Rexroth, from *One Hundred Poems from the Chinese*, copyright ©1970 by Kenneth Rexroth. Reprinted by permission of New Directions Publishing Corp.

Holly McNish, 'Soup Kitchens', from *Papers* (2012), published by Greenwich Exchange Ltd © Hollie McNish.

Portia Nelson, 'Autobiography in Five Chapters, from *There's a Hole in my Sidewalk: The Romance of Self-Discovery*. Copyright © 1993 Portia Nelson. Reprinted with permission of Beyond Words/Atria, a division of Simon & Schuster, Inc. All rights reserved.

Gil Scott-Heron, 'The Oldest Reason in the World', from *Now and Then*. Reprinted with kind permission of Canongate Ltd.

Lemn Sissay, 'Flushed', from *Gold from the Stone: New and Selected Poems* (2016), copyright © Lemn Sissay, published by Canongate Ltd. Reprinted with kind permission of Lemn Sissay.

Tracy K. Smith, 'Sci-Fi', from *Life on Mars.* Copyright © 2011 by Tracy K. Smith. Reprinted with the permission of The Permissions Company, Inc. on behalf of Graywolf Press, Minneapolis, Minnesota, www.graywolfpress.org

Kate Tempest, 'The Point', from *Hold Your Own* (2014), published by Picador Poetry © Kate Tempest.

All shall be well
and all shall be well
and all manner of thing
shall be well.

Dame Julian of Norwich